HEALTH MATTERS

UNDERSTANDING

CANCER

BY

HOLLY DUHIG

PowerKiDS press

New York

Published in 2019 by The Rosen Publishing Group
29 East 21st Street, New York, NY 10010

Copyright © 2018 Booklife Publishing
This edition is published by arrangement with Booklife Publishing

Edited by: Kristy Holmes
Designed by: Drue Rintoul

Image Credits
All images are courtesy of Shutterstock.com, unless otherwise specified. With thanks to Getty Images, Thinkstock Photo and iStockphoto.
Front Cover, 2 – Photographee.eu. 4&5 – Alila Medical Media, royaltystockphoto. com, Minerva Studio, Sergey Nivens. 6&7 – XiXinXing, Tyler Olson. 8&9 – Kluva, Kateryna Kon, Designua, Kateryna Kon. 10&11 – Image Point Fr, sciencepics, GraphicsRF. 12&13 – Olga Rudyk, T-Photo, YAKOBCHUK VIACHESLAV. 14&15 – frantab, Kateryna Kon, all_about_people, andriano.cz. 16&17 – A3pfamily, Photographee.eu. 18&19 – Chang-Pooh24, TinnaPong, JPC-PROD. 20&21 – thanongsuk harakunno, XiXinXing. 22&23 – JPC-PROD, Photographee.eu, DenisProduction.com. 24&25 – John Panella, Dimarion, ElRoi. 26&27 – Monkey Business Images, Gladskikh Tatiana. 28&29 – royaltystockphoto.com, Lightspring. 30 – De Visu, photogeoff.

Cataloging-in-Publication Data

Names: Duhig, Holly.
Title: Understanding cancer / Holly Duhig.
Description: New York : PowerKids Press, 2019. | Series: Health matters | Includes glossary and index.
Identifiers: LCCN ISBN 9781538338551 (pbk.) | ISBN 9781538338544 (library bound) | ISBN 9781538338568 (6 pack)
Subjects: LCSH: Cancer--Juvenile literature. | Cancer--Treatment--Juvenile literature.
Classification: LCC RC264.D84 2019 | DDC 616.99'4--dc23

Manufactured in the United States of America

CPSIA Compliance Information: Batch CSPK18: For further information, contact Rosen Publishing, New York, New York, at 1-800-237-9932.

CONTENTS

Words that look like **this** are explained in the glossary on page 31.

WHAT IS CANCER?

Cancer is actually a name for a group of diseases that affect the body's cells. Cells are the basic building blocks of our bodies and the bodies of all living things. There are many different types of cells in your body, each with different jobs to do. Some carry oxygen through your blood, some send messages between your body and your brain, and some group together to form organs such as your heart, lungs, and liver.

It is the job of all cells, however, to help keep you alive. Healthy cells do this by dividing and making copies of themselves in a controlled way that helps us to grow, heal, and repair. Cancer is caused by unhealthy cells making copies of themselves in a way that is not controlled. These unhealthy cells group together to form something called a tumor.

CANCER CELLS

NORMAL CELLS

FACT

THERE ARE AROUND 210 DIFFERENT TYPES OF CELLS IN THE BODY, AND THEY ALL HAVE DIFFERENT JOBS.

CANCER TUMOR

Lots of people will either have cancer, or will know someone who does, at some point in their lifetime. Because of this, cancer gets talked about a lot on the news and doctors are always trying to find new and better ways to treat it.

Cancer is a serious disease because, if it is not treated or if it spreads very quickly, it can be **fatal**. However, nowadays people can be treated quickly and more people are recovering from cancer than ever before.

Even though it is more common in adults, children can be **diagnosed** with cancer, too. However, although cancer is a serious illness, many people get better from it and go on to lead healthy lives.

TESTING FOR CANCER

If a doctor believes that someone has cancer, that person will usually need to have lots of tests done to find out for sure. This means that they will probably need to make many visits to the hospital. This is often worrying for the family and friends of someone with cancer, but it's important to remember that these hospital visits are a good thing because they are all about trying to make people better.

Testing for cancer might include blood tests, where a doctor will take some blood from a vein in your arm and send it away to be tested by experts. Other types of tests include X-rays and MRI scans. These scans give doctors a very detailed image of the body which will show them if there are any tumors.

X-rays and MRI scans do not hurt and are very useful for doctors. The sooner cancer is found during these tests, the easier it is to treat. If, after testing, someone is diagnosed with cancer, they will be taken care of by an oncologist (on-KAH-luh-jist) - a doctor that specializes in cancer treatment. Because cancer can be quite a complicated illness, an oncologist's first job will be to explain to their patient everything they need to know about their diagnosis. This includes where in their body the cancer has been found and whether or not it has spread to other parts of their body.

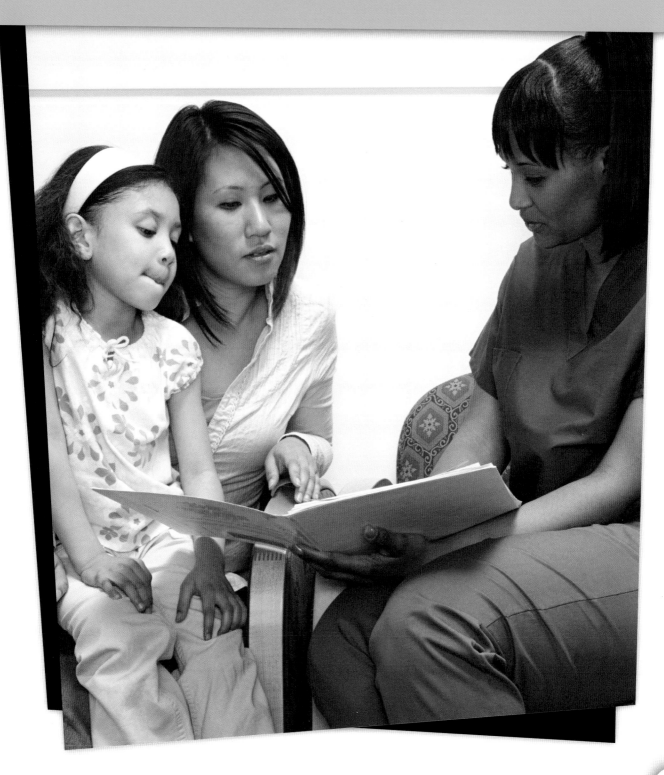

CELLS AND TUMORS

Being diagnosed with cancer, or knowing someone who has, can be worrying for anybody of any age. However, understanding more about what cancer is, how it develops, and how it's treated can help it to feel less frightening and more manageable.

TUMORS

Benign Tumors

Some tumors are considered benign (be-NYN). This means that they are not cancerous. These tumors grow slowly, don't spread, and are surrounded by lots of healthy cells that help contain them.

HARMLESS BIRTHMARKS, ALSO CALLED HEMANGIOMAS, ARE A TYPE OF BENIGN TUMOR.

Malignant Tumors

Malignant tumors are cancerous, which means they grow out of control and are able to spread to other parts of the body. But why are these tumors so damaging to our health?

One way in which a tumor can cause damage is by destroying nearby healthy cells. For example, if a malignant tumor began in someone's liver (the organ that cleans the blood), it might destroy the healthy cells around it and stop the liver from working. All cells, including unhealthy cells, need a supply of oxygen and **nutrients** to stay alive. To get this, cells are able to send out signals that tell the body to start making blood **vessels**. With a blood supply, a tumor can keep on growing and growing.

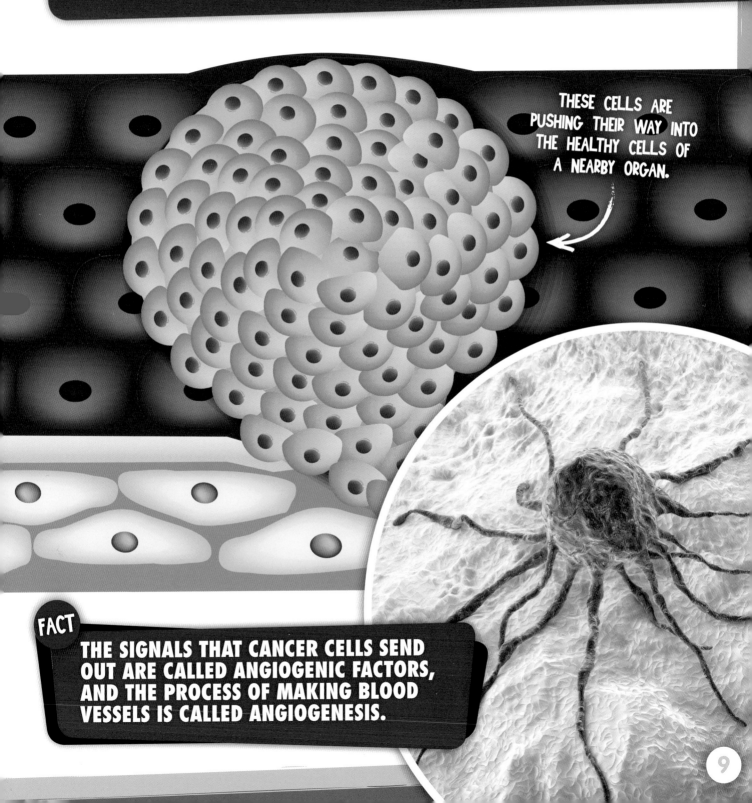

THESE CELLS ARE PUSHING THEIR WAY INTO THE HEALTHY CELLS OF A NEARBY ORGAN.

FACT

THE SIGNALS THAT CANCER CELLS SEND OUT ARE CALLED ANGIOGENIC FACTORS, AND THE PROCESS OF MAKING BLOOD VESSELS IS CALLED ANGIOGENESIS.

HOW TUMORS SPREAD

Circulatory System

Cancer tumors are able to spread around the body in many ways. One of these ways is through the system of blood vessels, veins, and **arteries** called the circulatory (SUR-kyoo-luh-tor-ee) system. As cancer tumors grow bigger, they press on nearby healthy cells. As they do this, they squash the blood vessels that supply the healthy cells and cause them to starve.

This makes it even easier for the tumor to spread. Cells from the tumor may also break off from the first tumor – also known as the primary tumor – and travel through the blood vessels. Because all the blood vessels and veins in the body are connected, the cancerous cells are able to spread through the whole body.

Lymphatic System

Cancer is also able to spread through the lymphatic (lim-fa-tic) system. This system uses vessels to take away waste, such as extra fluids and bacteria, and destroy it in places called lymph nodes. Like the circulatory system, the lymphatic system also reaches all over the body. However, it is made of much smaller vessels. Sometimes these vessels pick up and try to destroy cancer cells. Your body does this to try to protect you but it can provide another way for cancer to spread.

LYMPHATIC SYSTEM

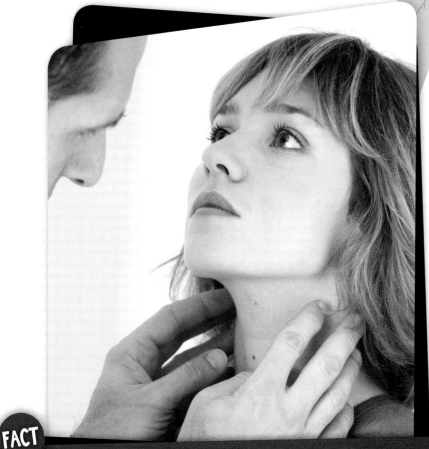

FACT

WHEN CHECKING FOR CANCER, DOCTORS OFTEN CHECK FOR SWOLLEN LYMPH NODES IN THE NECK.

TYPES OF CANCER

Cancer is more common in adults than in children. As people get older, their cells are not as good at dividing and growing. When children do get cancer, there are some types that are more common than others. One in every four children who have a tumor have it on their brain or **spinal cord**. These tumors are usually noncancerous. However, we don't call them benign because, even though they aren't cancer, they can cause damage to very important parts of the body.

BRAIN

SPINAL CORD

Brain Tumors

A brain tumor can have lots of different symptoms depending on where in the brain it grows. If it grows in the cerebrum – the part of your brain that controls emotions, language, and some movements – it can cause symptoms such as **seizures**, speech problems, and **paralysis**. The spinal cord is responsible for sending signals from your brain to your body and back again. How much of the body is affected by a spinal cord tumor depends on how far up the spine the tumor is found.

MRI SCAN OF A BRAIN TUMOR

FACT

DIFFERENT TYPES OF CANCER HAVE DIFFERENT SYMPTOMS BECAUSE THEY AFFECT DIFFERENT PARTS OF THE BODY.

LEUKEMIA

Leukemia (loo-KEE-mee-ya) is a cancer that affects the blood-making cells in our bodies. Blood is made in the soft, inner part of our bones, called our bone marrow. In the bone marrow, there are lots of cells called stem cells, waiting to be turned into blood cells. There are two types of blood cells: red blood cells and white blood cells. Cell **fragments**, called platelets, are also made in the bone marrow. White blood cells travel through our bodies and help fight off germs and infections. Leukemia is a cancer of these white blood cells. It means that the body is making lots of **faulty** white blood cells that can't do their job properly. When these cells grow out of control, they stop the body from being able to make red blood cells. Red blood cells are important because they carry oxygen around the body.

LEUKEMIA WHITE BLOOD CELLS

ONE IN EVERY THREE CHILDREN WHO ARE DIAGNOSED WITH CANCER HAVE LEUKEMIA.

FACT

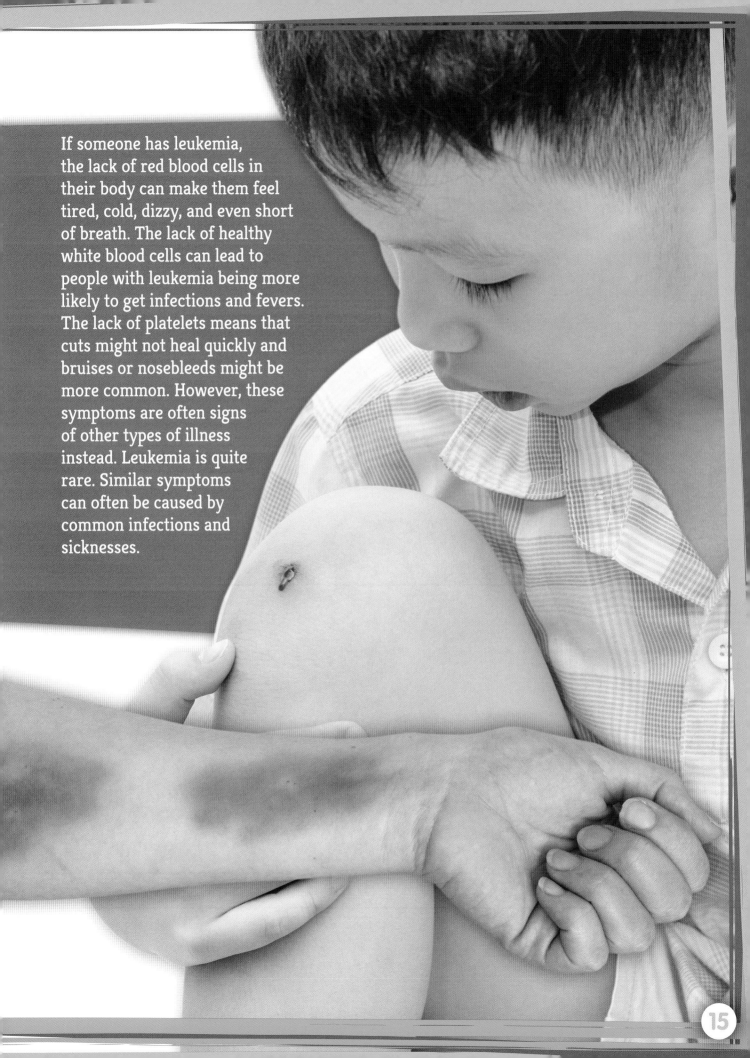

If someone has leukemia, the lack of red blood cells in their body can make them feel tired, cold, dizzy, and even short of breath. The lack of healthy white blood cells can lead to people with leukemia being more likely to get infections and fevers. The lack of platelets means that cuts might not heal quickly and bruises or nosebleeds might be more common. However, these symptoms are often signs of other types of illness instead. Leukemia is quite rare. Similar symptoms can often be caused by common infections and sicknesses.

TREATMENTS

There are lots of treatments for all types of cancer and these are constantly being improved upon by doctors and scientists. One of the main treatments for cancer, which most people have heard of, is called chemotherapy (kee-mo-THER-uh-pee), often called chemo (kee-mo) for short. Chemotherapy is a type of cancer treatment that uses drugs and medicine that are cytotoxic, which means cell-killing.

There are many different types of chemotherapy drugs and many ways they can be delivered to your body. Some chemotherapy drugs are given straight into your veins. This can be done at the hospital using a cannula. This is a tube which goes into a vein in the back of your hand or arm, and is taken out by a doctor before you go home.

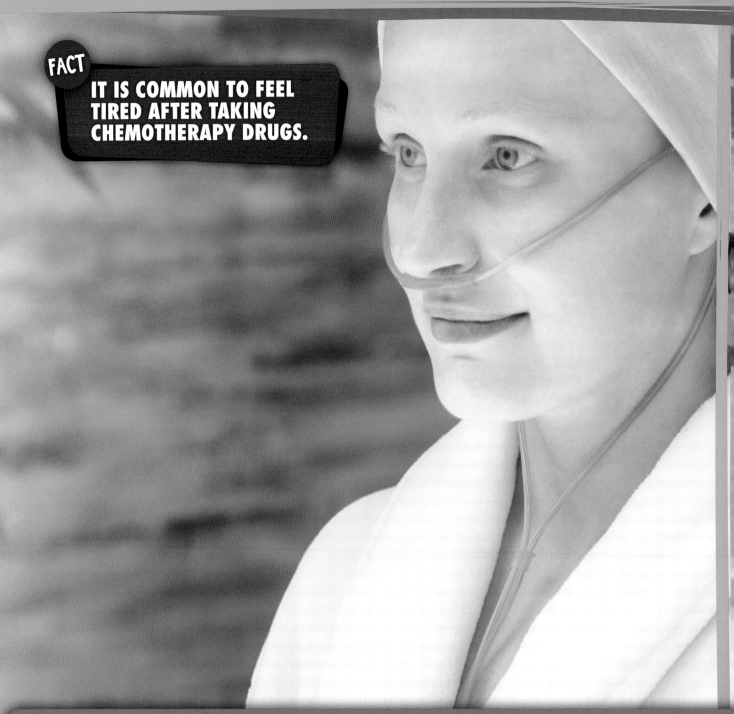

IT IS COMMON TO FEEL TIRED AFTER TAKING CHEMOTHERAPY DRUGS.

There are also ways of delivering chemotherapy drugs to patients at home. This allows people who have cancer to get on with their normal day-to-day lives while being treated. One of the most common ways of treating cancer at home is through a pump that is connected to a patient's arm or chest. This pump can be carried in a bag or on a belt.

A doctor or nurse will teach the patient, as well as their family or caregivers, how to take care of their pump at home. Other chemotherapy treatments include having injections into the fluid around the spine and taking drugs orally (by swallowing them). This is often done to treat brain tumors and leukemia.

SIDE EFFECTS

Chemotherapy kills cancer cells, but it also kills healthy cells, too. This can lead to lots of **temporary** side effects. One of the most noticeable side effects of chemotherapy is hair loss. Hair loss is often thought to be a symptom of cancer, but it is actually a side effect of cancer treatment. Hair loss happens because chemotherapy kills the cells under the skin that make hair grow. For both children and adults with cancer, losing their hair can often be quite upsetting. However, it's important to remember that hair loss is only happening because of drugs that are helping people get better.

FACT

SOME PEOPLE WITH CANCER GET SHORT HAIRCUTS OR USE HEADSCARVES, HATS, AND WIGS TO HIDE THEIR HAIR LOSS, WHILE OTHERS DON'T. IT IS ALL ABOUT PERSONAL CHOICE.

It is also common for people having cancer treatment to have a sore mouth. This is because chemotherapy is designed to kill fast-growing cancer cells, but it also affects the fast-growing, normal cells in the mouth. This can make the inside of the cheeks, gums, and throat hurt, and can even cause a loss of appetite. This can cause people who are going through treatment to worry, but it is actually a very normal thing to happen and is a sign that the chemotherapy is doing its job.

YOU CAN STILL DO NORMAL THINGS, SUCH AS GO TO SCHOOL OR STUDY, DURING CANCER TREATMENT. THIS BOY IS DOING HIS HOMEWORK WHILE HE IS IN THE HOSPITAL.

CASE STUDY: MIRANDA

My name is Miranda. I am nine years old and I have leukemia. I had been feeling bad and tired for a while before I was diagnosed by my doctor. Mom and Dad took me to the doctor when my tummy started looking **bloated**. The doctor explained that I was feeling tired because my body was trying to fight cancer and that it was the cancer that was making my tummy swell up. I didn't really know what cancer was at first but I knew it was serious. My doctor explained it to me very well and that helped me understand what was happening.

My treatment included chemotherapy as well as lots of blood transfusions, which is where a doctor puts blood from a **donor** into my body so that I don't run out of red blood cells. My treatment seemed to go on forever and it was very difficult at times. I kept thinking that it wasn't fair. Why did I have to get cancer? My friends were very nice, but having cancer made me feel different. Because of this, I saw a **counselor** who helped me talk about how I was feeling.

I was going through treatment for a long time but eventually my cancer started getting better. I still have to go to the hospital for checkups and treatments to make sure the cancer doesn't come back, but things seem to be improving.

I WORE A HAT DURING MY TREATMENT TO COVER MY HAIR WHEN IT STARTED FALLING OUT.

TALKING ABOUT YOUR FEELINGS

Having someone close to you be diagnosed with cancer, or being diagnosed yourself, can be an emotional experience. Some people with cancer feel scared or even angry. Nobody deserves to be ill, and it can feel very unfair when you or someone you love gets sick. Talking to someone you trust, like a parent or caregiver, can help you to feel better. Some people also choose to talk to a counselor. Some counselors are experts in helping people who are going through illnesses like cancer.

FACT

KEEPING A DIARY OR WRITING LETTERS TO YOUR LOVED ONES CAN HELP GET THE FEELINGS THAT ARE IN YOUR HEAD OUT ON PAPER.

If you have cancer, it can help to talk to other people who are going through it, too. Some hospitals will have **support groups** where you can talk to people the same age as you who are going through similar treatments.

When someone close to you has cancer, you might feel like you don't want to add to their worries by talking to them about yours. This might stop you from talking openly about how you feel. However, talking openly is helpful for everybody; it can let your loved ones know that you care and that you are there for them. Talking can also help the friends and families of people with cancer to share their worries.

MORE TREATMENTS

Radiation Therapy

Radiation therapy is a type of cancer treatment that uses high-energy X-rays or **gamma rays** to shrink tumors and kill cancer cells. Unlike chemotherapy, which affects the whole body, radiation therapy affects the tumor directly. This means it can focus on the tumor cells and not damage as many healthy cells. It can also help shrink cancer tumors that are causing blockages in the body. For example, a tumor in the lungs can make breathing and exercising very difficult, so radiation therapy could help to shrink or kill the tumor so that the patient feels better.

Stem Cell Transplants

Stem cells, like the ones in bone marrow, are a type of cell that don't have a specific job. They are very useful in treating cancer because they can be made into any type of cell the body needs. Stem cells can be given to a cancer patient by a donor and they can help your body to recover after treatments like chemotherapy and radiotherapy. Stem cell transplants are especially useful for treating leukemia because, when injected into the blood of a cancer patient, the donor's healthy stem cells can attack the patient's cancer cells.

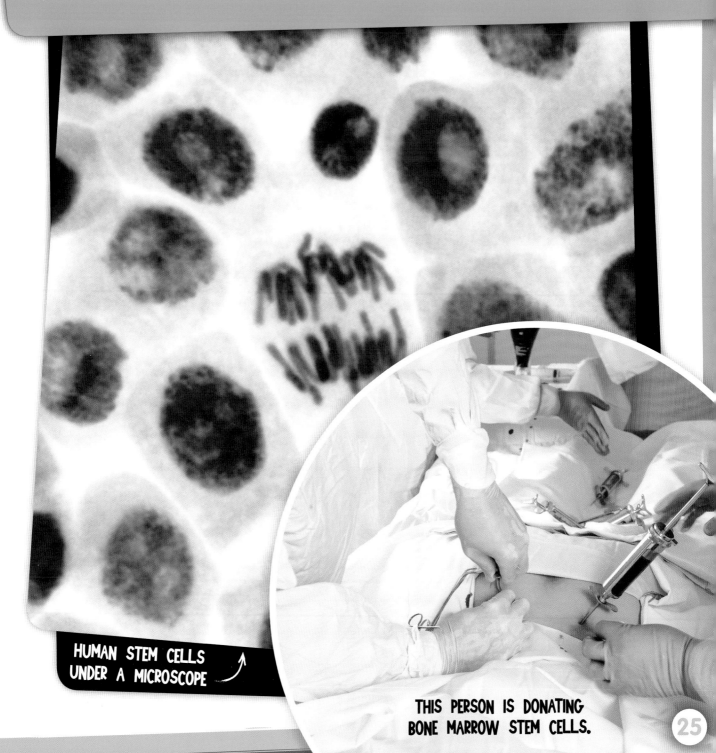

HUMAN STEM CELLS UNDER A MICROSCOPE

THIS PERSON IS DONATING BONE MARROW STEM CELLS.

CASE STUDY: CHRISTINA

My name is Christina and my mom's name is Julie. My mom used to have cancer. The doctors say she is in **remission** now which means the doctors can't find any more cancer in her body. When my mom was sick, I felt really scared. I couldn't concentrate on my schoolwork because I was so worried about my mom. I used to get scared whenever anyone talked about cancer at home and I would run upstairs to my room. I just wanted everything to go back to normal.

One day my mom took me to the hospital with her so that I could meet the doctors who were taking care of her. They told me about everything they were doing to try to help my mom's cancer go away. The doctor told me that my mom was a very strong lady and that her body was fighting cancer really well. They told me that my mom had breast cancer but that it hadn't spread anywhere else and that this was a good sign. I felt much less scared after talking to the doctor. Mom had chemotherapy as well as an operation and now she is much better. Her hair has even started growing back! This year we are both doing a **sponsored** run to help raise money for cancer charities.

CANCER RESEARCH

Cancer affects many people and their families. Because of this, lots of research has been done into finding newer and better treatments for it. Scientists are hopeful that new research and technology will lead to more effective cancer treatments and maybe one day even a cure.

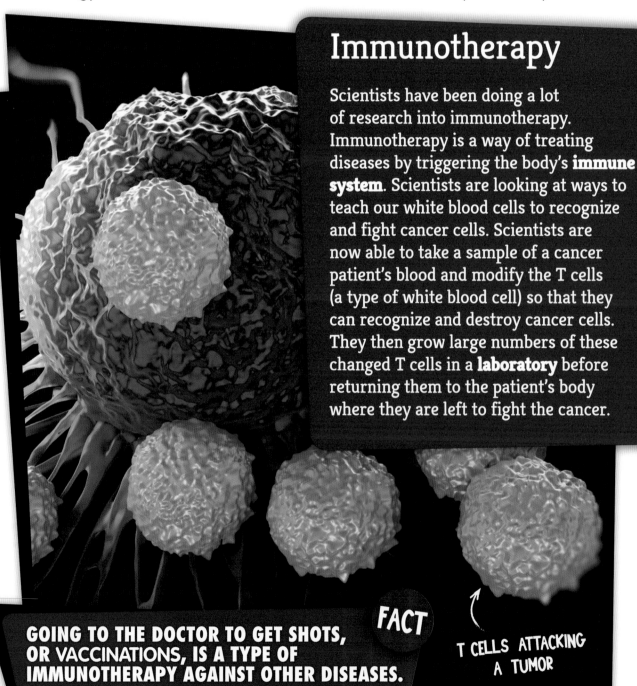

Immunotherapy

Scientists have been doing a lot of research into immunotherapy. Immunotherapy is a way of treating diseases by triggering the body's **immune system**. Scientists are looking at ways to teach our white blood cells to recognize and fight cancer cells. Scientists are now able to take a sample of a cancer patient's blood and modify the T cells (a type of white blood cell) so that they can recognize and destroy cancer cells. They then grow large numbers of these changed T cells in a **laboratory** before returning them to the patient's body where they are left to fight the cancer.

FACT

GOING TO THE DOCTOR TO GET SHOTS, OR VACCINATIONS, IS A TYPE OF IMMUNOTHERAPY AGAINST OTHER DISEASES.

T CELLS ATTACKING A TUMOR

Nanotechnology

Nanotechnology is technology smaller than 100 **nanometers**. Scientists are working on developing nanoparticles that can attach to cancer tumors and deliver chemotherapy drugs to them without harming the rest of the body. Scientists also hope that, instead of delivering drugs, nanoparticles can be sent to tumors and then heated by lasers until they explode. This explosion will be so small that it will only kill the cancer cells, and not the healthy cells around it.

DONATIONS AND FUNDRAISING

Cancer research takes lots of time and needs lots of money. None of these lifesaving discoveries would be possible without donations and fundraising from people who want to find a cure for cancer faster. There are lots of charities all around the world that are set up to care for people affected by cancer or to help fund research projects to find cures for cancer.

People all over the world do all sorts of weird and wonderful things to raise money for charities. Some people organize sponsored events such as walks, marathons, or talent shows. Some people shave their heads to raise money and show support for loved ones going through cancer treatment. Why not see if you can get involved? See if there are any events taking place in your area. If not, why not ask an adult to help you organize a fundraising event?

GLOSSARY

arteries   tubes that carry blood away from the heart and to the rest of the body

bloated   swollen with fluid or gas

counselor   a person who is specially trained to listen and give advice

diagnosed   when a disease or illness is identified by a doctor

donor   a person who donates their healthy blood, organs, or stem cells to help others

fatal   able to cause death

faulty   not working or made correctly

fragments   tiny, broken pieces

gamma rays   a type of electromagnetic radiation

immune system   the body's defense against illness

laboratory   a room or building used by scientists to conduct experiments and research

nanometers   units of measurement equal to one billionth of a meter

nutrients   natural substances that people need to grow and stay healthy

paralysis   being unable to move part or all of your body

remission   a decrease in or disappearance of signs and symptoms of cancer

seizures   sudden uncontrolled electrical activity in the brain

spinal cord   the cord of nervous tissue that extends from the brain and through the backbone

sponsored   to support a person, organization, or activity by giving money

support groups   groups of people with similar experiences who come together for support and comfort

temporary   only lasting for a short time

vaccinations   treatments designed to make someone immune to a certain disease

vessels   tubes in the body

INDEX